The Longest Midnight

By D’Amoretti Teddy Seussa

ISBN: 9 781387 618

Table of Contents

Dewdrop

Dewdrops keep falling as tears
Touching the ground, something beautiful comes up.
In the middle of this pain, crying hard and freely
Not ashamed to weep ‘cause the heartache is too much.
A slow, steady flow of aching sprinkled in the anguish
Poured out on the earth
Those flowers blossom into the scent of victory.

Parallel Universe

Awkward schedule running off-kilter
Existing in a universe parallel to the world.
Time is sped up quicker than before.
Is it just me? Have I been living in another time zone?
If you have seen clocks hanging upside down on mantles
Maybe you know about time running awry.
It's coming to a head; I need to sit and breathe.
Until then, I will watch vigilantly
For time to stop hyperspacing and slow down.

Short

Now a word from our frozen minds

Locked inside a hollow body.

A still, solid form, longing to speak.

It awaits the semblence of something

Something small or something tall,

Unsure of what anymore.

It is too soon to tell what exactly happens

When the footwork comes instead.

Is it over, or too late for me to say?

I don't know what it is anymore.

It is too much to say,

Too much to think about.

I don't have any more words to breathe.

They are sprawled out there

Waiting for life to begin.

Life

For a second, I breathe.

In a minute, I stand still.

For an hour, I walk alone through lonely valleys.

In a day, I wait.

In weeks, I hold on to hope.

In months, I don't give up.

In years, I don't forget who I am amongst the shadows of this land.

I cannot let go of the joy which reaches my soul

Oh, down to the core.

I cannot regret the choices made.

I am not the mistakes.

I am not the lost cause.

I am going on, I am moving forward.

I am not alone.

I am putting together, running up against all kinds of weather

Whether or not I like it.

It is not a fancy, it is not a passing hobby.

It is life, and I must take it on

Ready or not.

Hanging Words

Every day is getting shorter or longer, nonetheless.

It depends on what you believe

Of the science of breaths.

Some can't stand the thought of living in a pattern, confined to order in the stagnancy of time,

And would choose to unsyncopate the lines.

As conversation dawdles, as buses come out of yellow lines,

The stories are driven by running dialogues in silence.

Every moment is a blurb, a word pasted on a screen.

Can you make heads or tails of anything?

Running miniature creatures, blowing dandelion petals;

Sunsets and sunrises, coming up and down the skies.

Oh, I am a sitting muse, waiting for my cues along the side.

Until I make an entrance, I observe and listen patiently to the world's never-ending sighs.

The corners come up tautly in a sunbeam's smile

While the awkward talk runs on, a babbling brook of rhymes

Unmetered in iambic pentameter, wallowing in sorrows nowhere in their lives.

As you read a blog on your smartphone, I sit down with a book,

Pouring over its pages, thousands of times I have looked.

You speak to it incessantly, cursing something stone-faced,

Something that won't give you ears or eyes, or share in your opines.

In the frigid conversation, in the staggering lines, oh how time flies!

If the world is indeed an oyster, and we are called its pearls,

Can we offer up wisdom worth sharing with our future boys and girls?

We rotate new ideas, with our philosophies and theologies, making sense of everything,

Then dash them on the rocks

Once confronted with difficulties.

Still, with our long-winded conversations, our empathies and whines, so it is with our lives.

Hanging up words with the sheets, amongst the common village gossip dangling in the street,

Interpreting the signs and signals portrayed in pantomime whilst we ponder side by side.

There lies the texted chatter, splattered quickly in such shrines, little portraits of our times.

Indigo

Does anyone know what indigo is? Can anyone tell me?
The shadow behind the skies, watching beyond the clouds.
The song in the lonely hours, pouring out in sorrowful tones.
When moments of sadness overflow, there is nothing left but billows
Rolling in the deepest sea, mysterious, boundless depths of searching.
Indigo, what can you be?
A flower exploding petals, the richest of hues,
Dewy sighs of delight, morning, evening, and noon.
Evening draws on her silky garments, shimmering for her dance
Under the candlelit beams, wearing her pearls into the late hours.
Indigo, who are you?
Are you waiting for me?

Two Points

My brain got lost between two points,

At the intersection of here and now.

I worked to find it, but it's nowhere to be found.

Where or how it happened, I can't say for sure,

But I lost my mind; I must be either crazy or wild.

I am scavenging among ruins; faded dreams, lost glory days

I can't relive with relish.

I must relinquish them from my existence.

I am a misfit toy; no place for me to go,

Just search and believe this block shall move;

Incompetence, ignorance, impossibility, dissolving to nothing.

Hope, help, healing, enter tranquility;

From the chaos that was between the two points,

At the corner of five seconds and this moment.

I’m awaiting release after dauntlessly seeking relief

In the space between two points.

Hands

Hands to give or take,

To hold open or close upon the world.

Containing all I want inside; keeping out any possibilities.

Open hands to give what I have away.

Closed to clasp and claw the prospects,

Whittled down to nothing.

Opened, I awaken new days, new hopes, new dreams;

Closed, they disappear from sight.

Hands to choose my destiny.

Will I fulfill all I'm meant to in the months and years

Or limit my options as I feel best suited?

Hands to hold and hands to mold.

Hands to shape and hands that make the world a better place.

Hands that harm and hands that heal,

Hands that break and hands that seal a promise.

Hands to give or take.

Which ones will they be today?

I Wonder if You Wander

I wonder if you wander along the shore

While the tide rolls in and Time fades into gray.

I wonder if you wander when daylight pours its rays upon your face.

As your soul lays barren, washed up in the waves, you long for refreshment,

Though water is at your feet.

In the thousands of grains of sand, you wonder if someone will notice you

As they will notice me.

Somehow, we take each second for granted, the minutes to share our hearts with another.

In a breath and a sigh, it passes by

Too quickly; take each drop in when you can.

I wonder if you wonder when someone will carry you underneath wings of hope.

Does the suffering grieve your heartstrings so much that the sun won't shine tomorrow?

As you cry the next bottle of rain, you want to hide your head in the caves of Remorse.

You can't escape the past or run far enough for the dawn to catch you.

Don't lose sight; redemption has come.

Open your eyes and heart, for tomorrow is come.

I wonder if you wander the shifting sands of life,

The shoreline too long and the tide too high.

Waves crashing, undertow pulling into its side,

Wiping out all hopes of success, all joy in this world.

Tossing, turning, shipwrecked; sunken treasures, us boys and girls.

But with compression, the pressure in His hands,

He takes these challenges, turning us into His pearls.

Precious, priceless, perfected by trials on this lonely beach.

I wonder if you wander on this rock, on this isle.

Isolation and desolation; seeking not to be stiff and still

But full of vibrancy and brightness.

No one is an island; no one is a shore.

Love will restore and heal the broken.

Love is the ocean, and we are the sea;

Flowing, growing, feeding one another in plentiful, beautiful bounty.

On goes its continuous fount, the water that never runs dry for the parched heart.

I wonder if you wander along this shore,

Thinking and watching as Time rolls on.

But wait, don't lose heart, you can't give up now:

Hope is alive, it lives for tomorrow!

Trial by Fire

Trial by fire, burn me pure and clean

I want to stand up and be seen, without blemish

Real as can be; sure and steady in the sight of Thee

Sharpen, refine, hone this desire

Make me ready to be seen

That I may be strong and mighty

In the face of adversity

The Deep, Dark Side of Love

Tasting the deep, dark side of love

Though it is bitter, the seeds are impossible to swallow

I shall overcome the feeling I am nothing

'Cause I am something, taking a risk in the dark

Shining a light

Though the thoughts of hurt and hate attack from every angle

I have no fear of such piercings

I am coming out stronger

Your words and your silence won't scar my body

I am Teflon, I am resilient

You are leaving me nothing except stronger

Running

Running into the unknown
Unsure where to go
Falling, the light is flickering glimmers
I hold speckles and I run, hoping against doubts and fears
Though I have no exact calculations
No time or date stamped in perfect lettering
I go forth, bursting with all my might, taking each step in stride
Though the pain strikes my soles
Though it stings down to the marrow
I keep running
I can't give up until I climb the highest ground
When I run to the clouds, when I find refuge
I will seek You out, the source of my rescue
I will seek You now, and I know you carry me
In the shadow of your wings

Underground

Perhaps now is not the time to be unearthed.
Perhaps I enjoy being underground.
Perhaps I like the thrill of mystery;
Not everyone needs to know all the details.
Some words are best left unspoken,
And I like to guard my tongue; it is a loose thing,
Needing restraint against its aims to destroy me.
Perhaps you think I am too harsh a master,
But I need to be smart and mete out the weights
That come in bearing my image to the world; my real self, unbridled
But quick to see the false face that lies underneath the masquerade.
Perhaps you don't understand it yet or know what it means to live
In the light of reality.
So perhaps, someday, you will learn to light the world on fire
And know the song of joy.

Brokenness (We Don't Need Another Program)

Jagged, ragged deep breaths
Can hardly stand to draw them in
Tearing me apart inside; gravity falls upon my skull
I wonder if there is any room for me
Each pocket of air is getting thin; the walls are caving in
It is enough of a hassle, grappling with the shadows of sleep
When awakening from the dark; it is light that is fragile
A prism's beam that springs to life
I wonder if that's ever gonna change things
As we scramble toward the wreckage of our souls
We don't need another theorem; we don't need another path to roam
We only seek a place to run after Time collapses
When all is said and done

Swallows of sandstorms, strands of the former life
Thousands of castles in the air; all have come to ruins
Longings unfulfilled, desires forsaken; hours spent helpless, bruised by circumstances
While I wonder if there is any room for change
As we pull on doors, leading to destruction
We don't need another program
We only seek a place to run after broken things
When all is said and done

This world is full of confusion; no rest for the weary
When you think there's a solution, perplexity enters the side gate
Why do we try to go our own way?
We don't need another process; we don't love it in the wilderness
We only seek a place to run after Brokenness
When all is said and done

When all falls apart; when nothing is left to hold on to; when there is nothing left to do
When we have no more resolutions; when we are at wit's end, longing for a real friend
When we lose all pride in the world's eyes; when the state of our souls is barren and dry
When all is said and done
When all is said and done

Let Me Be A Woman

Let me be a woman who walks with integrity, head held high, not lowered in shame.
Let me be a woman who knows when to move, not stopping amid disorder and chaos.
Let me be a woman who knows what to say, never speaking opposite her actions.
Let me be a woman who shows mercy and forgiveness, not justice in my name.
Let me be a woman, a real flesh-and-blood woman who doesn't act like another.
A woman who thinks for herself, not an echo of collective thought.
Let me be a woman of truth, honesty outweighs a lie.
Let me be a woman who is one of a kind, a woman unlike the rest.
t me be a woman who, when put to the test, mettle for mettle is ready for the worst and the best
Not flimsy and failing to handle the pressure.
Lord, let me be a woman of strength and beauty from within
Outer beauty and strength fade in ages to come.
Let me be a woman full of hope and joy, even in the darkest days
Not full of despair or self-pity, weeping for yesterdays long gone.
Let me be a woman who is ready to move, unafraid to take a risk.
Let me be a woman who changes the world one moment at a time
Not Wonder Woman or Super Girl, burning out my energies.
But let me be a woman who is comfortable in my skin
Not acting some part in a play.
Lord, let me be a woman ready to stand and sing in the rain.
Smile when I am ready to cry, not out of false emotion but for the joy of living
May I be a woman
Who is loved and beloved by You?

Boundless Light

Light burst into a thousand flames
This spire of stars stirs up a thousand memories
Brilliant hope, emeralds descending on the sky
Untouched, a flicker of joy enmeshed in the darkness
Glowing amid sorrow, gleaming bits of happiness
The harbor beacons the better side, not the bitter side
Orbiting around the sun, gravitating about the glimmer of life
Shining forth from each point of the galaxy
All creation sings in praise the awesome magnitude of majesty
Drawing deep from spoken depths of space, boundless songs of praise
Ever on to eternity

May It Pass

Clouds fill the sky as tears form in my eyes
The void has come, taking over me
There is nothing left but shattered dreams
Look out, here comes despair, gusting in with her gales
Watch her blow, watch her swarm with a thousand winds of change
How the tides swirl, how anger bursts in peals of thunder and lightning
Striking hope down to the quick
Oh, may it pass with a breeze, not lingering.

Funnel clouds forming on the horizon, twisted situations enough to make me sick
The fields provide no shelter from the storm
It's gonna get hard, it's gonna get tough
One false move and I shall get caught up in the elements thrown my way.
Learn to adapt, be ready to break
Hit the ground with a bound, crying aloud with a great noise
Oh, may it pass with the greatest of ease, not lingering.

Sinking sand, shivering cold, blinking back the sting of sorrow
Ceaselessly struggling against sucking quicksand
I pull and push against these chains
An effort that longs for freedom
If it's gonna be a challenge, what's one more thing?
If this is torture, what's one more lashing?
Bring on the pain; I shall sing in prison
Unless I learn to smile despite hardships, shipwrecks, wreckage
I will never know the price of liberty
Oh, may it pass with peace, not lingering.

Oh, may the storms pass with relative calm, not lingering as a sore spot for my soul
May each wind, each hurricane, earthquake, and disaster come to pass
In calmness that they do not linger in bitterness, but betterness in my life.

Healing

Stars of cold, gray ice;
Matter dense and hard, granite-faced; the light of love is gone.
Where have you gone, oh Joy? Where have you run, oh Love?
Don't cast your shadow so far from here.
You are hiding during all this pain.
You keep me guessing the next destination your beam will shine;
I cannot bear the dark any longer than necessary.
Oh Hope, come shine through this prism of despair;
I long to see you there, awaiting me.
I am hungry, I am barren, I am wasted in this desert land.
I am seeking the sunshine, the help that comes for my soul.
I don't want to stay with Isolation; the desolation is wearing me out.
I need to taste the waters of life, to feel the rush of Freedom.
Come, let me know what it means to see, taste, to feel
Healing.

Hope is Dawning

Healing one bit at a time
Each moment passes as a second hand unwound
The sprockets are turning one for the other
Pouring forth blessings, hopes that cast out fears, doubts set aside
Nothing more but salt and light for the world to see
Despite the longest line of waiting
For dawn to break

Oasis

Wandered so long in the wilderness

Not a drop left to drink, not a thing to eat

I am dry, I am bone, emaciated and cracked

Gaunt is a compliment for this weary soul

I long for a spring of refreshment

Drop some rain, some cool, damp moisture on me

I seek refuge from this struggle inside

I am weary, I am restless, I am distressed

I want an oasis to rest, to set down all my burdens

While they wash down the river's side

I want to be saved and soothed

Your balm is the only thing that will heal me

Ten Years

Ten years go by so fast; ten years is a moment's past
Ten years is the blink of an eye, a breath, a second
It is mind-boggling, it is beyond me, it is a wonder how I got through it all
You were there, holding my hand in the darkest of nights, in the shade of the sun
cloaked me when I burned; you covered my shame as I turned into the lowliest of your beloved
I have no words left on my lips; I am quick to let these songs pour forth from my heart
I am not going to let this mountaintop overwhelm me
I stand in the sunlight, but I cannot be blindsided
Stumbling, then thrown off the course
I cannot let the high times be the striking point
The mark on which I hope to achieve always
I shall fall, I shall be hurt, I shall get scars
The healing, the sorrows that come are breaking down, which strengthens my bond with you
May I hold fast to all you are, not just what you do in me?

What can time be?
What are minutes but a glimpse into the past, portals of our history?
How can the hours run? Bits and pieces of a fragmented age
Honing into the second the world perplexed me
As I fell further into the rabbit hole, lost all sense of space, all sense of life
Nothing seemed to matter
as I dead? Did I breathe the same air? Would I fall down the shaft forever, staying in this state?
Trapped in the walls of silence, hearing my thoughts echo
Nothing answered back; not one thing in the cacophonous sound
Except your voice, softly comforting me
I felt alone; your warmth exuded
I still feel the coals touch my lips, pardoning me to speak
Your words of hope
In an isolated era

A Purple Haze

Can I make you walk a mile in my shoes?

Can I make you stand a minute, shaking as I sometimes do?

Can you feel a thunderbolt to the brain?

Can you know the years of memory loss?

Can you see the words come in picture frames?

Can you touch the scars of side effects in your blood

While moments pass by and awaken to another month of a purple haze?

Purple haze; the daydreams and thunderbolts, racing in the brain at lightning speed

The fog is thick, the way ain't clear; awakening unaware of the surroundings

Time goes too fast, the brain's scattered, and all that's left is fragments in these hands

Calmly, collectively, take each second as it comes in breaths

Can you prevent one from starting? Can you make one stop?

Can you control your surroundings at a manageable pace?

Can you make the weather change?

Can you walk out of a purple haze?

Purple haze; the daydreams and thunderbolts, racing in the brain at lightning speed

The fog is thick; tunnel vision sets in and all goes silent except the noise inside

Time ticks so quickly; the brain is in shards, scarred and battered to rest in these hands

Come find some rest, and refresh your soul in the stillness of silence

Can you find a cure for the disease?

Can you know why we have them?

Can you make life brighter than the purple haze?

Purple haze; the daydreams and thunderbolts, racing in the brain at lightning speed

e fog is thick; vertigo swirls the world, the brain's confused, seeking guidance from these hands

Time to find some peace and rest,

Calming such haggard breaths release

Upon the heart wanting quiet, wanting hope from the darkest days

That comes in the purple haze

Reflection

What have I done? What have I become?

This is not the woman I thought I'd be

I've transformed out of something sheltered, out of the shell I lived in

Not a frightened little girl, not a fragile child who fears the darkness of night

I can see the light that surrounds me, warm and enveloping each step I take

It is the tiniest movements that transform the heart

My mirror image has changed; the reflection is not so grim

Sooty or saturated with grime on the inside

I have come a long way from the hollowed woods

Don't want to return any time soon

I am moving forward; no time to glance back

I stand tall against the looking glass

Unafraid of my image anymore

Story

The story is unfinished, the cover not yet bound
The print is hard to read, and the language undetermined
The plot is difficult to follow, too much stream of consciousness
If you can decide the outcome from the slow peaks and great fails
Your guess is as good as mine
Knowing who I am in Christ is all I can see.
Everything else is a mystery.
The tale is under construction, the inkwell needs refilled
He is writing my story. I only interpret as best I can
I am limited by prejudices, and my story is not always true
Self obscures things from the panoramic view
I fill in what’s left behind
In time

Acknowledgements

"The Longest Midnight" is a term I came up with to describe the years I was at risk for Sudden Unexplained Death in Epilepsy (SUDEP) due to nocturnal seizures or seizures in my sleep. Every night before bed, my parents made sure I had "bumpers" set up so I wouldn't roll onto my stomach by accident. (Try NOT doing that in your sleep!) I also had a bell by my bed in case I needed assistance in the middle of the night. It was a long season. Going to sleep was difficult during those years. I'd sometimes wonder if I'd sleep without seizures or wake up in the morning. Cooking and writing became my therapeutic outlets. I enjoyed seeing my Grammy P and the moments we would share baking and talking about recipes. I wrote down lots of my thoughts during the longest midnight. I also had some very dear friends and family who stuck with me during this season and the aftermath. I would love to acknowledge them.

Brittany, Ashly, Stephen, Matthew, Breanna, Hope, Barbie, Kathryn, Rachel, and my epilepsy community: You all are some of the dearest people I know. I am so grateful you came alongside me, especially when so much of the time felt like big brain fog. I am so glad you are in my life. Thanks for being part of the journey!

My Jayfest crew—Michael, Jay, Janelle, Kevin, Kevina, Kevin S., Jacob, Nathaniel, Joey B., Joey L., Christian, Marco, Amy, David, Miriam, and countless other folks in this wonderful community—I am so glad I am learning about you and growing with you. I thank you for wanting to learn more and be more present in these moments!

My editor, Sarah: I would be pecking away through many midnight hours oblivious to mistakes without your keen eyes and good ear for rhythms. Thank you for your friendship and aid. I appreciate you so much!

My family: I love you guys so much! Thanks for your support over the years, even when you had no idea what I was saying half the time. Thanks for sticking with me.

This book is made in loving memory of my late Grammy P: baking buddy, awesome Grammy, sewing genius, musician, artist, and all-around woman of integrity. I miss you and I am so glad you were part of my neighborhood!

- Every year, 50,000 people die from Sudden Unexplained Death in Epilepsy (SUDEP). There is no cure for it, and the reason why this happens to some folks affected by epilepsy is unknown. I lost three friends to SUDEP and was at risk for it myself for three years of my epilepsy journey. If you are interested in learning more about epilepsy and the risk of SUDEP, please check out this site www.theepilepsynetwork.com.

About the Author

'Amoretti Teddy Seussa is a disabled poet, spoken word poet, and writer. She has written nine oks, including two under her real name. She was featured on the podcast *The Spoonie Authors etwork (SPAN)* hosted by Dianna Gunn and published by Silent Sparks Press for their Summer ᵓoetry collection called *Astounding Poetry*. She also has a YouTube Channel called Purplexity epsy. You can find more of her work and merchandise on Facebook, Commaful, WordPress, and Patreon.

WordPress: www.plasmnetic.wordpress.com
Facebook: www.facebook.com/purplelology
Patreon: www.patreon.com/epivision
Commaful: www.commaful.com/damorettiteddy
YouTube: www.youtube.com/purplexityepilepsy

www.ingramcontent.com/pod-product-compliance
Ingram Content Group UK Ltd.
Pitfield, Milton Keynes, MK11 3LW, UK
UKHW051133260726
13967UKWH00010B/3023